MEET THE COMMUNITY HELPERS!

A DAY WITH A DENTIST

by Mari Schuh
illustrated by Dean Gray

GRASSHOPPER

Ideas for Parents & Teachers

Grasshopper Books introduce children to fiction at the earliest levels. Fun storylines and easy-to-follow text support early readers as they learn to read informational fiction and enhance their imagination. Sight words, repetitive sentence patterns, and fun illustrations support early readers.

Before Reading

- Discuss the cover illustration. What do they see?
- Look at the picture glossary together. Discuss the words.

Read the Book

- Read the book to the child, or have him or her read independently.
- "Walk" through the book and look at the illustrations. Who is the main character? What is happening in the story?

After Reading

- Prompt the child to think more. Ask: Would you like to be a dentist? Why or why not?

Grasshopper Books are published by Jump!
5357 Penn Avenue South
Minneapolis, MN 55419
www.jumplibrary.com

Library of Congress Cataloging-in-Publication Data

Names: Schuh, Mari C., 1975– author. | Gray, Dean, illustrator.
Title: A day with a dentist / by Mari Schuh;
[illustrated by Dean Gray].
Description: Minneapolis, MN: Jump!, Inc., 2025.
Series: Meet the community helpers! | Includes index.
Audience: Ages 5–8
Identifiers: LCCN 2023046348 (print)
LCCN 2023046349 (ebook)
ISBN 9798892130899 (hardcover)
ISBN 9798892130905 (paperback)
ISBN 9798892130912 (ebook)
Subjects: LCSH: Dentists—Juvenile fiction.
Readers (Primary) | LCGFT: Readers (Publications).
Classification: LCC PE1119.2 .S37287 2025 (print)
LCC PE1119.2 (ebook)
DDC 428.6/2—dc23/eng/20231017
LC record available at https://lccn.loc.gov/2023046348
LC ebook record available at https://lccn.loc.gov/2023046349

Editor: Jenna Gleisner
Direction and Layout: Emma Almgren-Bersie
Illustrator: Dean Gray

Printed in the United States of America at
Corporate Graphics in North Mankato, Minnesota.

For Dr. Steven

Table of Contents

Caring for Teeth

Dr. Dena's dentist's office is full.

She has many patients to see.

Min's checkup is first.

"Hi, Min!" says the hygienist. "I'm Ross. I will clean your teeth before you see Dr. Dena."

The cleaning tool buzzes.

It tickles.

Ross took X-rays of Min's teeth.

Dr. Dena checks them.

She checks Min's teeth and gums, too.

Ed needs a tooth pulled.

Dr. Dena gives Ed a shot in his gums.

It numbs his mouth.

He won't feel pain.

She pulls the tooth out!

Siri has a cavity.

A cavity is a hole.

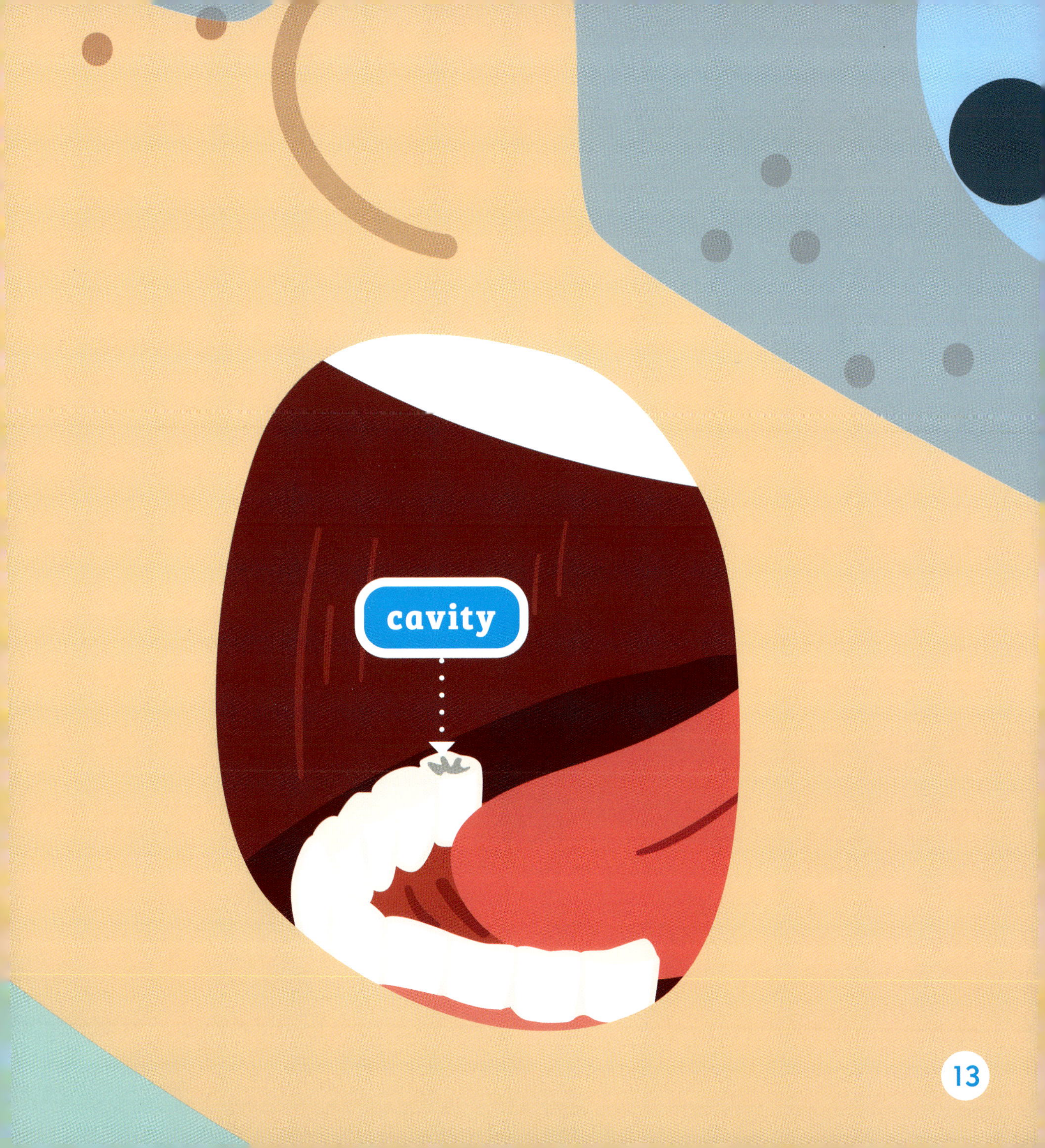
cavity

Dr. Dena puts a filling in the tooth.

It fills the hole.

It can't get bigger.

All better!

Leo is the last patient of the day.

Dr. Dena checks his teeth.

"You have a healthy smile," she says. "Keep up the good work."

She gives Leo a toothbrush to take home.

"Thank you, Dr. Dena!" Leo says. He smiles.

"Your next checkup is in six months. See you then, Leo!" she says.

Quiz Time!

How does Dr. Dena fix Siri's cavity?

A. She pulls Siri's tooth. **B.** She puts a filling in Siri's tooth.
C. She flosses Siri's teeth. **D.** She takes X-rays of Siri's teeth.

Dentist Tools

Take a look at some of a dentist's tools!

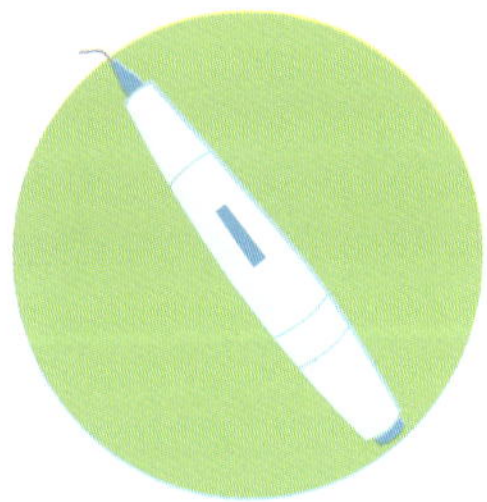

ultrasonic scaler

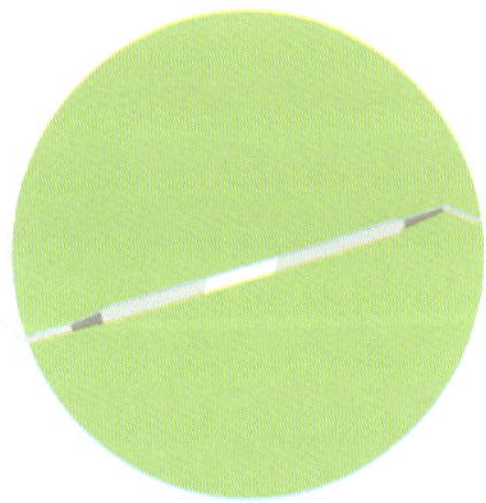

metal scaler

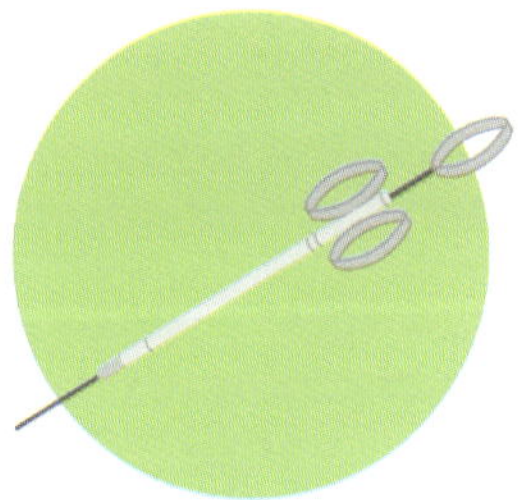

syringe

floss

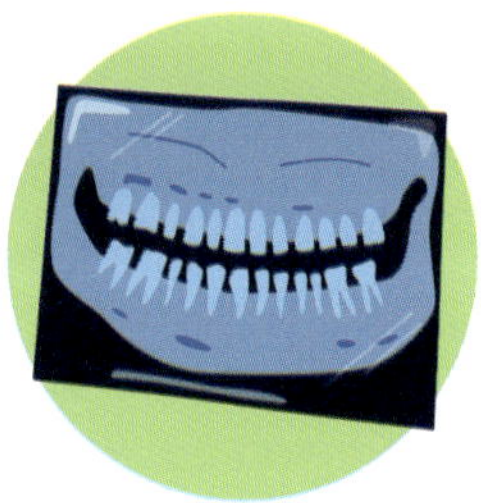

X-ray

mirror

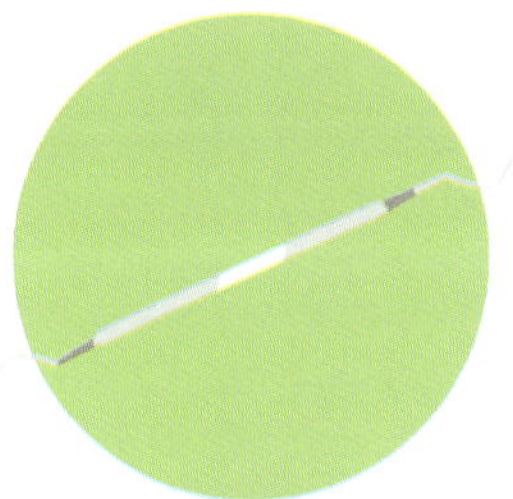

explorer

dental chair and light

Quiz Time! Answer Key: **B.** She puts a filling in Siri's tooth.

Picture Glossary

cavity
A hole in a tooth that is caused by decay, or rotting.

checkup
A visit to the dentist to make sure one's teeth, gums, and mouth are healthy.

gums
The firm, pink flesh around teeth.

hygienist
A person who is trained to clean teeth, take X-rays, and help dentists.

patients
People who get treatment and care.

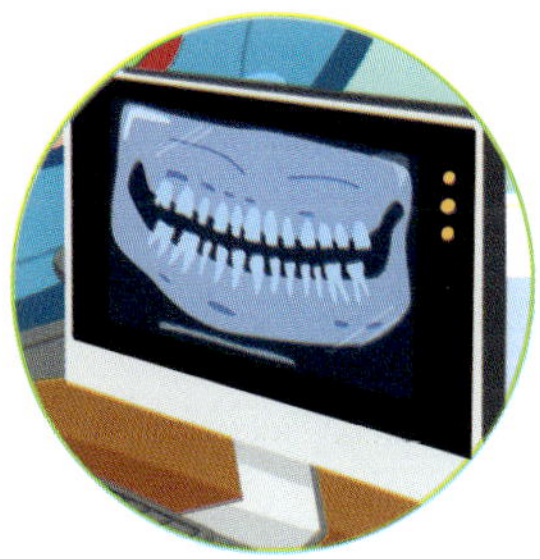

X-rays
Pictures of the inside of a person's mouth or body.

Index

To Learn More

FACT SURFER

Finding more information is as easy as 1, 2, 3.

1. Go to www.factsurfer.com
2. Enter "**adaywithadentist**" into the search box.
3. Choose your book to see a list of websites.